Tony Attwood

Oxford University Press
Music Department Ely House 37 Dover Street London W1X 4AH

In the early days of rock 'n' roll it was generally believed that there was only one correct way to perform a pop song, and that was the way it was sung and played on the record. However, in the 1960s a number of British pop groups started recording older American songs in new ways, and people began arguing as to which was the 'correct' way to play the songs — in the original American style or the new British way.

Gradually people came to see that there was no one 'correct' way of performing pop music. In the 1970s Bob Dylan started making new recordings of his most famous songs. Slow folk tunes became fast rock songs with complete rock group backing, and chord sequences, rhythms and even melodies were changed. Sometimes it was hard to recognize the original song!

Today most people accept that it is up to the performer to make what he or she can of a pop song, and the same is true in folk music (although some people do like to preserve earlier versions of folk songs so that they may be compared with modern versions).

For this reason you should see the music in this book as merely a set of themes waiting for you to organize some variations on them. No time indications are given for the songs because you should feel free to experiment. The melodies given here do not always correspond exactly with what you can hear on record. Sometimes this is because they have been changed to make them easier for young people to sing. But it also sometimes happens that a singer has chosen to change the melody to suit himself after the original music has been printed. This does not make one version right and another wrong. Study the printed music carefully, but then be prepared to modify what you find to produce the sort of music *you* want to create.

Acknowledgements

The author and publisher are grateful to the following London teachers for their help in compiling this material: Mrs. Kyle Abrahams, Sarah Siddons School, W2; Mr. Jan Anthonys, Mr. Charles Evans, and Mr. Piers Spencer, Woodberry Down School, N4; Miss Rita Carey, St. Richard of Chichester School, NW1; Mr. Ivor Cutler, Fox School, W8; Ms. Glynis Evans, Our Lady's Convent School, N16; Mr. David Ford, St. John's Primary School, SW9; Mr. Armand Julian, Chelsea School, SW10; Mrs. Rosie Mitchell, Wendell Park School, W12; Mrs. Babette Peterson, Ladbroke School, W10; Mr. Bob Smith, Haverstock Secondary School, NW3; Mrs. Susan Raynor, St. Paul's Way Secondary School, E3.

We are grateful to the following for permission to include their copyright songs:

Arnakata Music Ltd. ('Part of the Union' by John Ford and Richard Hudson);

ATV Music Ltd. ('Eleanor Rigby' by John Lennon and Paul McCartney © 1966 Northern Songs Ltd. for the world; 'Yesterday' by John Lennon and Paul McCartney © 1965 Northern Songs Ltd. for the world; 'Rivers of Babylon' by Farian/Reyam/Dowe/McNaughton © Far Musikverlag and Beverley Records for the world. © 1978 Far Musikverlag/Hansa Productions Ltd./ATV Music Ltd./Blue Mountain Music for UK & Eire; 'Downtown' by Tony Hatch © 1964 ATV Music Ltd. for the world);

Carlin Music Corporation ('Love me tender' by Elvis Presley and Vera Matson and 'Leftover Wine' by Melanie Safka);

EMI Music Publishing Ltd. ('Does your chewing gum lose its flavour?' by Lonnie Donegan © 1924 by Mills Music Inc., sub-published by B. Feldman & Co. Ltd., and 'If I were a Carpenter' by Tim Hardin © 1965 by Hudson Bay Music Co., sub-published by Robbins Music Corp. Ltd.; both songs reproduced by permission of EMI Music Publishing Ltd., 138-140 Charing Cross Road, London WC2H 0LD);

Essex Music International Ltd. ('Streets of London' by Ralph McTell and 'Killing me softly with his song' by Norman Gimbel and Charles Fox);

Dick James Music Ltd. ('Rocket Man (I think it's going to be a long long time)' by Elton John and Bernie Taupin © 1972 for the world by Dick James Music Ltd.);

McCartney Music ('Mull of Kintyre' by McCartney — Laine, Copyright © 1977 by MPL Communications Ltd. Administered by McCartney Music by arrangement with ATV Music Ltd.);

Southern Music Publishing Co. Ltd. ('Universal Soldier' by Buffy Ste Marie and 'Colours' by Donovan);

Tro-Essex Music Ltd. ('The Hammer Song' by Lee Hays and Pete Seeger);

Warner Bros. Music Ltd. ('Blowin' in the Wind' and 'When the ship comes in' both by Bob Dylan).

CONTENTS

Colours 4
Eleanor Rigby 6
Universal Soldier 8
Blowin' in the Wind 11
Wild Rover 14
Yesterday 16
Streets of London 18
Rocket Man 22
Killing me softly 25
Does your chewing gum lose its flavour? 28
Scarborough Fair 30
The hard times of old England 32
Careless Love 34
The Hammer Song 36
Love me tender 38
What month was Jesus born in? 40
Rivers of Babylon 42
Leftover Wine 46
Alabamy Bound 49
When the ship comes in 50
Downtown 52
Mull of Kintyre 54
If I were a Carpenter 58
Part of the Union 62

Colours was Donovan's second hit record, coming three months after *Catch the Wind*, in 1965. Like many of his songs it is basically very simple.

You may find that it is possible to work out some more verses in addition to the four that Donovan himself wrote. In the music you'll find that where there are no words in the song some notes have been printed in smaller type. They can be played by an accompanying instrument. A complete accompaniment suitable for glocks or xylophones is also shown.

Like many folk songs this song just consists of repeated verses. In order to make the song more interesting you might want to play one verse on tuned percussion instruments. To make this instrumental verse more interesting still you can actually play one verse of the song in a different key. In this case the song is written in the key of G major, and the instrumental verse in C major.

The complete song would then run as follows:

Verse 1	G major
Verse 2	G major
Verse 3	G major
Instrumental verse	C major
Verse 4	G major

The music you would play for a verse in C major is provided above.

Eleanor Rigby

Words and Music by
JOHN LENNON and PAUL McCARTNEY

Accompaniment for glocks and xylophones

Eleanor Rigby was a number 1 hit for the Beatles in 1966 — it was the last in a line of 11 consecutive number 1 hits in Britain for the group (their next release only got to number 2). The other side of the record, *Yellow Submarine*, was also a hit. Like many of the Beatles' songs of the time its lyrics are different from those of most other pop songs. *Yellow Submarine* is a fairy story, and *Eleanor Rigby* is about loneliness, whereas most pop songs are about love or dancing.

You will see that in bar 4 and again at the end of the piece, some notes are printed which do not have any words written underneath. These notes come from the accompaniment to the melody played on the recording of *Eleanor Rigby*. Because this accompaniment is a little difficult to perform it has not been used here, and a simpler version has been written out which can be played on glocks, etc. However, if you would like to try something a little harder, listen to the Beatles' recording of the song, and then try and work out an accompaniment that is similar to that on the record. The two short extracts given here will help you.

Projects

1 In this story of Eleanor Rigby what do we learn about her? What sort of person is she? What does she do all day? Write a story about a day in Eleanor's life, in which you make up scenes which are different from those told in the song.

2 What other records can you find that are not about love or dancing? Make a list of them and next to each record state what it is about.

Universal Soldier

Words and Music by
BUFFY Ste MARIE

He's five foot two, and he's six feet four; He fights with mis-siles and with

spears. He's all of thir-ty one, and he's on-ly sev-en-teen, Been a

sold-ier for a thou-sand years; He's a Cath-o-lic, a Hin-du, an

A-the-ist, a Jain, A Bud-dhist and a Bap-tist and a Jew; And he

knows he should-n't kill, and he knows he al-ways will Kill you for me, my friend, and me for

you. And he's fight-ing for Can-a-da, he's fight-ing for France, He's

fight-ing for the U. S. A., And he's fight-ing for the Rus-sians, and he's

fight-ing for Ja-pan, And he thinks we'll put an end to war this way, And he's

fight-ing for de-mo-cra-cy, he's fight-ing for the Reds; He says it's for the peace of all,

Universal Soldier is the most famous composition by an American Indian folk singer, Buffy Sainte-Marie. However, despite being well known, the song has never been a hit in Britain, although Buffy has had hits with songs such as *Soldier Blue* and *I'm gonna be a Country Girl again*.

The song contains a very strong anti-war feeling. Buffy Sainte-Marie suggests that there have always been ordinary soldiers fighting wars; whether they are fighting for a religion, a country or a belief the result is the same. And yet there is no need to have wars. The song ends by saying that if we all decided that there would be no more fighting we could put an end to violence now.

This song sounds particularly good if accompanied by a guitar playing the chords of the song, and a double bass, cello or bass guitar playing the bass accompaniment shown above.

Projects

1. In the song there are some words and references you might not understand. Explain the meaning of the following (if you are not sure, look up the words in a dictionary or encyclopedia):
    a) a Jain
    b) an Atheist
    c) a Buddhist
2. Find out what Buffy Sainte-Marie means by her reference to Hitler at Dachau.

Accompaniment for glocks, xylophones, and bass instruments

Blowin' in the Wind was one of Bob Dylan's earliest successes. Many people have recorded this song, and Peter, Paul and Mary and Stevie Wonder have had hits with it. Bob Dylan himself has continued to sing the song in his concerts, presenting it in many different ways, including a reggae version. You can play a reggae version yourself by placing a very heavy accent on the second and fourth note of each bar in an accompaniment. A simple accompaniment which can be used for a reggae version of the song is printed opposite. You can play the bass notes on a cello, bass guitar, double bass, or bass xylophone. The three notes in the chords can be played on glocks, xylophones, piano, etc.

Once you have mastered the style you can work out ways of varying the rhythm. Experiment with your friends until you find a rhythm that you like and that fits the song.

Projects

Discuss or write about these questions: What do you think the song is about? What is the answer that is blowing in the wind? Why does Dylan ask all these questions?

Wild Rover

Traditional
arranged TONY ATTWOOD

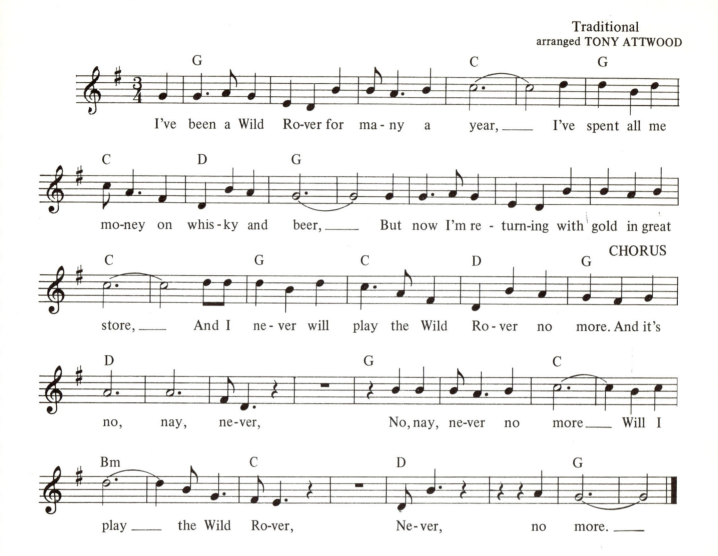

I've been a Wild Rover for many a year, I've spent all me money on whisky and beer, But now I'm returning with gold in great store, And I never will play the Wild Rover no more. And it's no, nay, never, No, nay, never no more Will I play the Wild Rover, Never, no more.

I went to an alehouse I used to frequent
And I told the landlady me money was spent.
I asked her for credit, she answered me 'Nay!
Such custom as yours I can get any day.'

CHORUS

I took out of my pocket ten guineas so bright
And the landlady's eyes, they were wide with delight.
She says 'Here is whisky and beer of the best,
And the words that I said, they were only in jest!'

CHORUS

I'll go home to my parents and confess all I've done
And I'll ask them to pardon their prodigal son.
And when they have done so — as oftimes before —
I never will play the Wild Rover no more.

CHORUS

Accompaniment for glocks and untuned percussion

Versions of this song have been found in many parts of the world including England, Australia and Ireland. Quite recently, the Dubliners made a record of it which went into the Irish charts, although the song has never been a hit in Britain.

A simple accompaniment for tuned and untuned instruments is given above. Even if you don't use any tuned instruments in the accompaniment you will need to do something during the rests that appear in three places in the chorus. The simplest thing to do is to clap your hands once for each percussion mark: ↓ . Alternatively, you might use tambourines or drums. A different accompaniment may be devised by playing the given accompaniment on a bass instrument such as a cello or bass guitar, and making the notes one octave lower than written.

Project

The last verse of the song mentions the 'prodigal son'. What did the prodigal son do? Where is the prodigal son mentioned other than in this song? In the original story of the prodigal son, what happened?

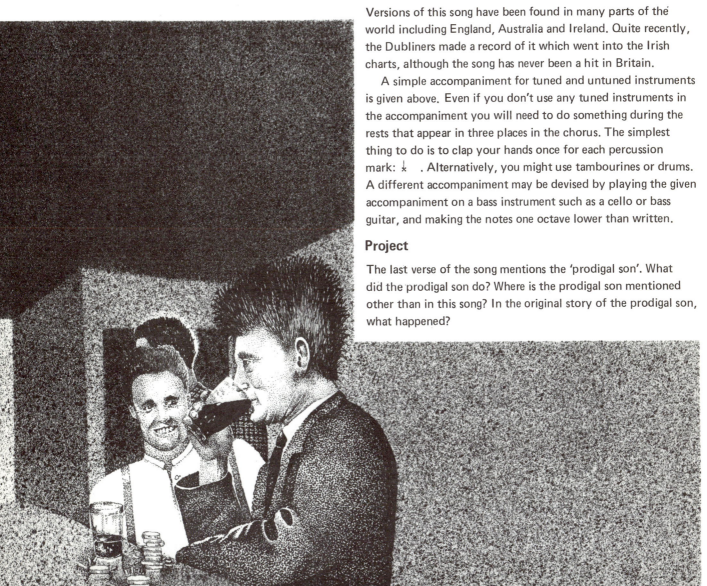

Yesterday

Words and Music by JOHN LENNON and PAUL McCARTNEY

Although the record and the music state that this song was written by John Lennon and Paul McCartney, it was in fact only written by Paul McCartney. It is probably the best of all his sad ballads. The story is very simple: a boy and girl are happy together, and then the next day the girl leaves, without the boy knowing why. Suddenly all his happiness is gone and he wishes the good times of Yesterday would return.

Paul McCartney has told a very interesting story about how he wrote this song. He states that he composed the tune one day, but couldn't find the words to go with it. In fact all he could think of for the opening bar was 'Scrambled eggs', which of course fits perfectly well instead of the word 'yesterday'. Eventually the words came to him. This shows part of the strength of this song; the words and music fit perfectly, and the tune itself seems to contain some of the sadness of the words.

Projects

1. Can you extend the lyrics? Try writing a new verse to *Yesterday*, starting with the word 'Yesterday' and then continuing through the next six bars.

2. One way in which *Yesterday* is rather unusual is the number of bars in the verse section — only seven instead of the usual eight, twelve or sixteen. Look through this book and see if you can find any other songs with an unusual number of bars in the verse.

Accompaniment for glocks, xylophones etc.

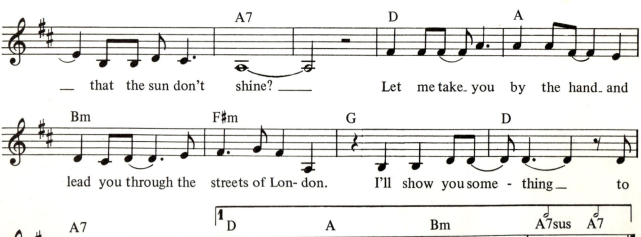

Accompaniment

INTRODUCTION

The song *Streets of London* was well known in folk clubs all over Britain for many years before the composer, Ralph McTell, had a hit with it in December 1974. Few people can fail to understand the meaning of the lyrics, for they represent a real situation. There are many 'down and outs' in all our big cities, who can be seen wandering around, sleeping in doorways, searching dustbins for food. It is because it is hard to know exactly what should be done about these people (if anything at all) that makes the song so meaningful.

But the song doesn't work only from the point of view of the lyrics. McTell has managed to write a song which combines some very unusual chords with a feeling that they all fit together. This is achieved through developing a simple descending bass line which will fit under the melody of the verses. This bass line is written out in the treble clef in the accompaniment for bars 9 to 14.

Some of the chords may be too difficult for you to play on the guitar. If so, use the following chart to change them into more common chords.

Written	Play
E9	E7
A7 sus 4	A7
A13	A7

Project

Look at bars 9 to 15 in the accompaniment. Play them on any instrument you like. Now work out a simple piece of music to fit around them; you may write it out or use an instrument to work out an improvisation. You may repeat the phrase as many times as you like. You should find it makes some interesting possibilities available, since in this form it is a 7-bar phrase rather than the more usual 8. When you have worked out your arrangement, play it through with someone else playing the original phrase.

Elton John's first hit record in Britain was *Your Song* — a hit in January 1971. However, it was not until April 1972 that he had his second hit single, *Rocket Man*, which got to number 2 in the charts.

Rocket Man is one of the few hit songs to deal with a subject from science-fiction. In this song the writers look to a future in which space travel has become commonplace. Being a spaceman is just another job, with its own disadvantages, such as loneliness.

Rocket Man is also unusual in that part of the song seems to be in a different key from the rest. It appears to start in D minor, but soon settles down into another key. What key is the song *actually* in?

As this song alternates between two keys a number of rather difficult chords are included, for instance B flat. Also, Elton John included certain chords (for example, suspended 4ths) which are moderately easy to play on the piano — the instrument Elton plays — but are more difficult on the guitar. To overcome the problem of the B flats it is possible to play the guitar accompaniment two and a half tones lower, with a capo fitted just below the fifth fret. This would mean that the first chord played would be A minor 7, and not D minor 7. Below are the chords used in the song. Complete the chart for the new chords:

Original	*With Capo under fifth fret.*
D minor 7	A minor 7
G 7	D 7
F	....
B flat	....
G minor 7 (sus 4)	....
C	....
G 9 sus 4	....
G minor 7	....
B flat 7 (sus 4)	....

An even better way of overcoming the problem of the complex chords is to ignore the last part of the chord name as follows:

> for a *minor 7*, play *minor*;
>
> for a *minor 7 sus 4* play *minor 7* (or, if you can't, *minor*);
>
> for a *9 sus 4* play *9* (or if you can't, *7*);
>
> for a *7 sus 4* play *7*.

Here is an example. If you don't know how to play G 9 sus 4 you could play G 9 instead, but if you can't play that either, you can play G 7. However, you will find all the chords written out on the back and front covers of the book, and you should take every opportunity to learn new chords and practise them in a song.

Beware! You *cannot* change a minor chord into a major chord just because the major is easier to play!

Projects

1 The lyrics of *Rocket Man* set a scene rather than tell a story. You are given information about a space traveller but not told anything of his adventures. Try and write a couple more verses to the song which in fact do give us some more information about this character.

2 Try and find some more pop songs which are about subjects taken from science fiction. Some songs written by David Bowie deal with this theme.

upper G
F#
F
E
―――――――――――――――――――――
D
D#
B
Bb
A
G
F#
F
E
―――――――――――――――――――――
D
C

```
G
F#
F
E
D
C#
C
B
Bb
A
G
F#
F
E
D
C
```

2. I felt all flushed with fever,
   Embarrassed by the crowd,
   I felt he found my letters and read each one out loud.
   I prayed that he would finish
   But he just kept right on.

   CHORUS Strumming my pain *etc.*

3. He sang as if he knew me,
   In all my dark despair,
   And then he looked right through me, as if I wasn't there.
   But he was there, this stranger,
   Singing clear and strong.

   CHORUS Strumming my pain *etc.*

Accompaniment for violins

This song was a hit for Roberta Flack in 1973, reaching number 6 in the British charts. It is remarkable for the unusual images of the lyrics, the equally unusual chord sequence, and the wide ranging melody.

What key is the song in? Clearly it starts in A minor (we can see this by the fact that there are no sharps or flats in the key signature and it starts with the chord of A minor). But by the fourth bar it seems to be in another key, and we may wonder if it actually did start in A minor. In bars 6 and 7 it seems to change again, and so on. Fill in the chart below for the key changes you suspect might be happening in this song.

Bars	Key
1– 2	A minor
3– 5	....
6– 7	....
8– 9	....
10–13	....

Now look at the verse — what key is that in? (Here's a clue — it stays in the same key from 'I heard he sang' to 'a stranger' after which it suddenly changes.)

A simple violin accompaniment is given to this song. If you feel you could handle something more complex develop this by putting in some passing notes between the semibreves. If you're unsure how to do this look back to some of the other songs in this book and see how the accompaniments are written out. You'll find it is often done by making the accompaniment play notes from the chord that is being played on the guitar.

Here's a suggestion for the first bars of the accompaniment:

 *etc.*

Compare this with the accompaniment given and see how it has been developed. Then try and continue it.

Project

Describe in an essay or story the experience of the singer of this song. Continue the story to take it past the end of the song. What happens next?

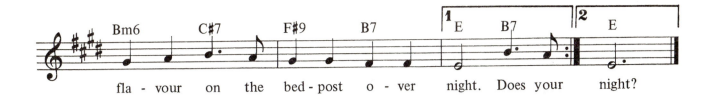

fla - vour on the bed-post o - ver night. Does your night?

Although few teenagers today will have heard of Lonnie Donegan he remains one of the ten most successful artists in terms of British pop chart success, since the charts were introduced in the 1950s. His first hit record was in 1956 and his last to date (his 33rd) was in 1962. *'Does your chewing gum lose its flavour?'* came in 1959, and reached number 3 in Britain. It was also an enormous hit in the United States.

Donegan was best known as a performer of skiffle. This was a simple type of rock 'n' roll played on acoustic guitar, a plucked bass instrument made from a wooden tea chest and broom handle (with a string tied from the end of the handle to the tea chest), drums (which could be more tea chests turned upside down), and an old-fashioned washboard rubbed with thimbles on the player's fingertips.

The idea was to create music which anyone could play. It cost very little to set up a skiffle group and the skills required were not very difficult to pick up — most skiffle players simply taught themselves. However, as time went by some of the skiffle groups started using more complex instruments, such as a double bass, an electric guitar and complete drum kit. The songs also became more elaborate and, as you can see from this song, instead of just using very simple chords on the guitar, more complex chords were introduced.

Project

Find out as much as you can about skiffle music. You will find quite a lot about skiffle in *Pop Music* by Michael Burnett (O.U.P.), or in an encyclopedia of pop music. You might also be able to find some recordings of skiffle by Lonnie Donegan. (But beware! Donegan did record some songs later in his career which were not skiffle at all.) Then try and perform your own version of a skiffle song using very simple instruments. You could make a tea chest bass, and tea chest drums, although it will be harder to find a wash-board. You could also try and do arrangements of non-skiffle songs in the skiffle style.

Scarborough Fair

Traditional
arranged TONY ATTWOOD

(Boy) Where are you going to? (Girl) Scar-bo-ro' Fair.

(Boy) Give my res-pects to a girl who lives there.

(Boy) Tell her to buy me the best yard of cloth,
And make me a beautiful shirt thereof.

Tell her to make it with a gold ring,
Stitch it and sew it without a seam.

Tell her to wash it in yonder well,
Where never a drop of water yet fell.

Tell her to dry it out by the sea,
And when it's dry, come give it to me.

(Girl) Oh where are you going to?
(Boy) Scarboro' Fair.
(Girl) Give my respects to a boy who lives there.

Tell him to buy me an acre of land
Between the salt sea and the sea sand.

Tell him to plough it with a deer's horn,
Sow it all over with one peppercorn.

Tell him to reap it with a sea fowl's quill,
Tan it all up into an eggshell.

And when he has completed his work,
Come unto me and he shall have his shirt.

Scarborough Fair is a very old folk song that exists in many different forms. One of the best known versions today is that recorded by Simon and Garfunkel, who changed the title to *Parsley, Sage, Rosemary and Thyme*. Early versions of the song had references to other place names, instead of Scarborough Fair, and included lines written in local dialect. For example, one early version read:

> 'Oh where are you going?' 'I'm going to Lynn.'
> Fellow ma la cus lomely.
> 'Give my respects to the lady therein,'
> Ma-ke-ta-lo, ke-ta-lo, tam-pa-lo, tam-pa-lo,
> Fellow ma la cus lomely.

In that version the girl went to Lynn and the boy to Japan.

Project

Because the song itself is very simple it is possible to build up improvisations on the theme. Learn to play the melody on a recorder, glockenspiel or other similar instrument and then play it through with some slight variations, so that you can build up an improvisation on the theme.

Three sets of accompaniments are given. These may be played separately, in pairs, or together.

The hard times of Old England

Traditional
arranged TONY ATTWOOD

1. Come all brother tradesmen that travel alone.
Oh, pray come and tell me where the trade is all gone.
Long time I have travelled and cannot find none.
And it's oh, the hard times of old England,
In old England very hard times.

2. Provisions you buy at the shop, it is true,
But if you've no money there's none there for you.
So what's a poor man and his family to do?
CHORUS

3. If you go to a shop and you ask for a job,
They will answer you there with a shake and a nod.
So that's enough to make a man turn out and rob.
CHORUS

4. You will see the poor tradesmen a-walking the street
From morning till night for employment to seek,
And scarcely they've got any shoes to their feet.
CHORUS

5. Our soldiers and sailors have just come from war,
Been fighting for queen and for country this year,
Come home to be starved, better stay where they were.
CHORUS

6. And now to conclude and to finish my song,
Let us hope that these hard times they will not last long.
I hope soon to have occasion to alter my song,
And sing: Oh, the good times of old England,
In old England jolly good times.

Accompaniment for violins or glocks

Alternative version of song

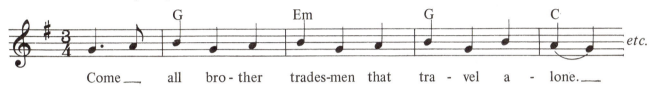

Come — all bro-ther trades-men that tra-vel a-lone. —

Many versions of this traditional folk song exist, most of the early ones being in 3/4 rather than 4/4 time. The chord sequence written alongside many modern versions also differs from version to version. The one given here is chosen as it allows the simple descending accompaniment to be used with it. The accompaniment may be played one octave higher if desired.

A modern version of this song with pop accompaniment appears on the Steeleye Span LP *All around my Hat*.

Project

Under the accompaniment you will find the start of another version of this same song, in 3/4 time. Try and continue it, making sure all the words fit to the new music you are writing.

Careless Love

Traditional
arranged TONY ATTWOOD

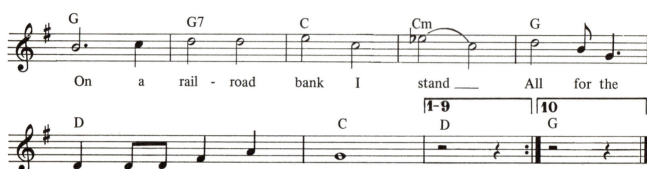

CHORUS *(after each verse)*
It's love, oh love, oh careless love,
It's love, oh love, oh careless love,
Love, oh love, oh careless love,
See what love has done to me.

I love my mama and papa too, *(three times)*
I'd leave them both to be with you.

Sorrow, sorrow to my heart *(twice)*
Oh sorrow, sorrow to my heart,
Since my love and I did part.

I cried last night and the night before, *(three times)*
I'll cry tonight but I'll cry no more.

Lord I wish that train would come, *(twice)*
Oh I wish that train would come,
To take me back from where I came from.

Careless Love is one of the earliest American folk blues, and should be sung in a gentle relaxed way. Unlike many of the later blues tunes it runs to 16 bars, not 12. In the traditional 12-bar sequence the chords in G major would be:

G G G G; C C G G; D7 C G D7;

(each chord here representing one bar of four beats).

Project

This is the sort of song that invites the singer to go on making up more and more verses; try and invent some yourself. You can also try and make up both the melody and words to a 12-bar blues accompaniment by the chord sequence given above.

Accompaniment

land. _____
land. _____ 2. If I had a
land. _____ 3. If I had a land. _____
        4. Well, I got a

Chords for reggae version

Accompaniment for glocks, xylophones or piano

This is one of the many songs which most people seem to know, although few can remember who had a hit with it. In fact it was Trini Lopez, an American singer who recorded it in 1965. However, many other people have recorded the song, often with changes in the melody, so it's quite possible that you have previously learned a different version.

The Hammer Song is a perfect example of how it is possible to write a successful, memorable tune which is very simple. There are four verses, each sung to the same 16-bar melody. It should offer encouragement to anyone who has thought that he or she could write a song.

If you feel you would like to try, then do — but keep it very simple. You may want to team up with a friend, with one of you writing the lyrics and the other the music. You may start with the lyrics or the melody or a chord sequence played on the guitar or piano. Above you can see an accompaniment for *The Hammer Song* for glocks or xylophone or piano. It could also be played by violins. You could also play the whole melody on these instruments, making it an instrumental verse to be played between verses 3 and 4.

Project

You will also see five chords written out. These can be used to play a reggae version of the song, using either a piano or bass guitar and glocks. In the music for the melody you will see, as usual, the names of the chords written above the music. If you want to write out the reggae accompaniment you should use these chord names and the chart of chords for the reggae version as follows:

1. Find the chord above the melody line.
2. Look to see how that chord is written out in bass and treble.
3. Now write it out in full in the reggae rhythm. In the treble this will be with the three notes on the second and fourth beats, and in the bass with the note on just the first beat. An example is given below, and a complete reggae accompaniment is given with the song *Blowin' in the Wind*.

Love me tender

Words and Music by
ELVIS PRESLEY and VERA MATSON

VERSE

1. Love me ten-der, love me sweet; Ne-ver let me go. You have made my life com-plete,
2. Love me ten-der, love me long; Take me to your heart. For it's there that I be-long,
3. Love me ten-der, love me dear; Tell me you are mine. I'll be yours through all the years,
4. When at last my dreams come true, Dar-ling, this I know. Hap-pi-ness will fol-low you

CHORUS

And I love you so.
And we'll ne-ver part.
Till the end of time.
Ev-'ry-where you go.

Love me ten-der, love me true, All my dreams ful-fil. For, my dar-lin', I love you, And I al-ways will. And I al-ways will.

Accompaniment

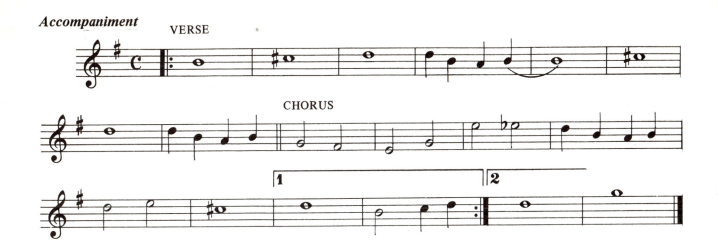

VERSE

CHORUS

This was not one of Elvis' greatest hits (it reached number 11 in 1956 — one of seven hits by Elvis in Britain that year), but it is remembered because of a film in which Elvis sang the song.

It is a lesson in how to write a very simple but very effective song. There are two sections (verse and chorus) each of 8 bars. There is some contrast between the two; the chorus starts off by repeating one note nine times, whereas the verse has more variety at the start. The chorus also uses chords that don't occur in the verse.

However, although the song is simple, it does contain a surprise in each section. Both in the verse and chorus the second chord (A7 in the verse, B7 in the chorus) is one that would not normally be expected in the key of G major. It's not the same chord each time — that would make it too obvious; so it is unusual enough to make the listener take notice, and not repeated so often as to become commonplace.

Project

Try and write a song with the following structure: a verse of eight bars followed by a chorus of eight bars. Keep the melody and chord structure simple. Make sure the listener can immediately distinguish between the chorus and the verse.

What month was Jesus born in?

Traditional
arranged TONY ATTWOOD

2. He was born of a virgin mother . . .

   CHORUS

3. He was laid in an oxen manger . . .

   CHORUS

4. His mother's name was Mary . . .

   CHORUS

Accompaniment

This is a song that is covered in mystery. It is hard to know exactly how old it is, and many different versions already exist, with more being made up all the time.

Many songwriters have tried to use the idea of a song that includes a list of all the months of the year. For example, there was *Calendar Girl* by Neil Sedaka, plus all the songs that use the name of just one month of the year, and the enormous number of Christmas songs, from carols through to humorous pop songs.

Projects

1. Make a collection of songs in which the lyrics deal with one or more months of the year. Are all the months treated in the same way?
2. Write a song in which the lyrics are about either one month of the year or about Christmas.

Accompaniment

Rivers of Babylon was a number 1 hit in Britain for the group Boney M in 1978, the fifth in a series of hits which started the previous year with *Daddy Cool* (which reached number 6 in January 1977). In fact, on the reverse side of *Daddy Cool* was *No Woman no Cry*, which you will find in Pop Songbook 2.

It is the form of the song *Rivers of Babylon* that makes it particularly interesting, for rather unusually for a popular song it has three sections: *A B* and *C*, with *A* then repeated. In addition there is an introduction and a coda.

Project
Answer these questions:

Where does the introduction begin, and end?
Where does section A begin and end?
Where does section B begin and end?
Where does section C begin and end?
On what section is the introduction based?

Accompaniment for strings

Leftover Wine was written by Melanie Safka, but has never been a hit in this country. It is a sad song about memories which the singer sees as the leftovers of the past. It needs to be sung slowly and with a lot of feeling for the lyrics.

For guitarists who wish to avoid the difficult chords involved in playing the song in E flat major optional chords are placed alongside the chords in E flat. These chords shown in brackets will fit with the melody if a capo is fitted to the guitar between the second and third frets.

The strings' accompaniment written here is quite easy to play and it may be that you would like to try something a little harder. In that case you can add some passing notes to the accompaniment as in this extract from the first few bars below:

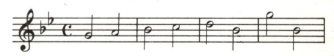

Compare this with the original and see if you can continue it.

Alabamy Bound

Traditional
arranged TONY ATTWOOD

Don't you leave me here, don't you leave me here,
But if you must go, then please just go,
Leave me a dime for beer.

I'm Alabamy bound, I'm Alabamy bound,
If the train don't run, I got a mule to ride,
I'm Alabamy bound.

Way down the road somewhere, way down the road somewhere,
I got a long tall girl that loves me still,
Way down the road somewhere.

This negro song has changed in the way that so many such songs have changed over the years. Originally it was a harsh and bitter song, sung by wandering negroes looking for work. The original lyrics reflected a tough view of life with many references to alcohol, sex and violence. In many early versions of the song the first and last lines are repeated, so that when a singer chose to perform the song very slowly he could emphasize the whole tedious process of wandering from town to town.

Later the song became used by white singers too, and verses such as the following were used:

If your hair don't curl, and your eyes ain't blue,
And you don't want me sweet Polly Anne
Then I don't want you.

which turned into a different sort of song.

The Alabamy of the title, is of course Alabama. Where is Alabama? Can you find other songs about Alabama?

Project

Take the new verse written above ('if your hair don't curl' etc.) and write a few more verses which continue the song in that way. Then perform the song, first using the older words given in the four verses at the top of the page, and then using the new lyrics you've just written. How should each song be performed? Should one be much slower than another? Would you want to make any melodic changes for the new words?

49

When the ship comes in

Words and Music by
BOB DYLAN

1. Oh, the time will come up When the winds will stop And the breeze will cease to be breath-in' Like the still-ness in the wind 'Fore the hur-ri-cane be-gins, The ho-ur when the ship comes in. Oh, the seas will split And the ship will hit And the shore-line sands will be shak-ing, Then the tide will sound And the wind will pound And the morn-ing will be break-ing.

D.S. three times

2. Oh, the fishes will laugh
   As they swim out of the path,
   And the seagulls they'll be smiling,
   And the rocks on the sand
   Will proudly stand
   The hour that the ship comes in.

   And the words they use
   For to get the ship confused
   Will not be understood as they're spoken,
   For the chains of the sea
   Will have busted in the night
   And will be buried at the bottom of the ocean.

3. A song will lift
   As the mainsail shifts
   And the boat drifts on to the shore line,
   And the sun will respect
   Every face on the deck
   The hour when the ship comes in.

   Then the sands will roll
   Out a carpet of gold
   For your weary toes to be a-touchin',
   And the ship's wise men
   Will remind you once again
   That the whole wide world is watchin'.

4. Oh, the foes will rise
   With the sleep still in their eyes
   And they'll jerk from their beds and think they're dreamin',
   But they'll pinch themselves and squeal
   And know that it's for real
   The hour when the ship comes in.

   Then they'll raise their hands
   Sayin' we'll meet all your demands,
   But we'll shout from the bow your days are numbered,
   And like Pharoah's triumph
   They'll be drownded in the tide
   And like Goliath they'll be conquered.

Counter-melody for glocks etc.

When the ship comes in comes from a very early LP by Bob Dylan, *Times they are a-changing*. When he first recorded this song Bob Dylan played the only accompaniment used on the record — a guitar and a 'blues' harmonica. The 'blues' harmonica is different from a chromatic harmonica in that it doesn't have a complete range of notes. If you buy a chromatic harmonica you can play in any key. But with the 'blues' harmonica you need to buy a particular instrument for the key you are playing in.

One of the important features of this instrument is that it will play two chords at the bottom end of the range — one when blown and one when sucked. A third chord can be achieved by sucking towards the top of the harmonica. In order to get the three chords mostly used in this song (G C and D) you could use a harmonica in G which gives the chord G when blown, and D when sucked at the bottom end of the range. The chord C can be gained by sucking at a certain point towards the top end. If you can, get a blues harmonica in G and work out a simple accompaniment to this song.

Project

All the songs on the album are about things that Dylan felt were very important when he recorded them. What do you think this song is about? What does the ship represent? What is it that makes the foes of the ship so afraid, in the last verse?

This is one of 27 hit records that Petula Clark has had since June 1954 when she first entered the British charts with *The little Shoemaker*. *Downtown* itself reached number 2 in 1964, and is one of those songs that has remained popular, often being requested on the radio even today.

The song centres around the word 'Downtown', which, every time it comes, involves a jump downwards of either a perfect 4th or a minor 3rd. This is a very clever piece of songwriting, since most people, having heard the song just once or twice, will be able to remember, and possibly sing, the word 'Downtown'. And as every songwriter knows, if the audience can remember just one part of a song, the song is very likely to be successful. You might find it hard to sing the opening three bars of the song accurately after hearing them just once or twice. But you will certainly remember the two notes that go with the word that makes up the title of the song. This means you might be very likely to go to a record shop and ask for a copy of this record.

The accompaniment given can be played on any bass inst- instrument, such as a bass guitar, bass xylophone, cello, etc., or the piano.

Project

Choose a very simple title for a song — one that only uses two or three words. You can use a poem you know — or write the lyrics to a song yourself if you wish — or just choose the title, and not worry about any other words. Now write a simple phrase of music to go with the title — try and make it as simple as the two note accompaniment to the word 'Downtown'. Having done that, try and build the rest of the song around that simple phrase. If you have lyrics for the rest of the song, set them to music. If not, write an instrumental piece.

Mull of Kintyre is one of the best-selling British songs of all time. It is another perfect example of how to make a simple idea into a very effective popular song.

It is particularly interesting to see how different it is from *Yesterday*, which was also written by Paul McCartney. Where *Yesterday* is complex (for example, in the chord sequence) *Mull of Kintyre* is simple. Yet both are descriptive songs — this one describing a place, and *Yesterday* describing a feeling of loneliness and regret.

Projects

1. Where is Mull of Kintyre? Find it on a map.
2. Do you know of any other songs that are about places? There are some in this book. Make a list of them. Draw a map showing these places.
3. *Mull of Kintyre* is unusual for a pop song in that it is in $\frac{3}{4}$ time. Find some other pop songs in $\frac{3}{4}$.
4. This song modulates (changes key). What key does it start in, where does it modulate, and to what key?
5. Play the chorus of *Mull of Kintyre* on a piano or glockenspiel. (The chorus is the first 12 bars of the melody.) You'll see how straightforward it is. Try and write a melody that is as simple and effective as this one. Note that the melody leaps up in the first bar and then takes the next 3 bars to come down to where it started. See if you can use the same sort of pattern.

Write the song in the key of C major, in $\frac{4}{4}$ time starting on the E above middle C.

If I Were a Carpenter

Words and Music by
TIM HARDIN

If I were a car-pen-ter and you were a la-dy, would you mar-ry me an-y-way would you have my ba-by.

If a tin-ker were my trade, would you still find me car-ry-ing the pots I made fol-low-ing be-hind me.

Save my love through lone-li-ness, save my love for sor-row, I've gi-ven you my on-li-ness

This song was a hit in Britain in 1964 for the Four Tops and in 1968 for Bobby Darin; in both cases the record got into the Top Ten. The composer of the song, Tim Hardin, who died in 1980, only had a very brief time in the charts himself — one week in the top 50 with *Hang on to a Dream*. Many of his songs have been recorded by others, including *Reason to Believe* which was recorded by Rod Stewart along with *Maggie May* in 1971, and got to number 1.

Project

If I were a Carpenter uses a straightforward chord sequence which is to be found in many pop and blues songs. This takes the form of *tonic* chord, *flattened 7th* chord, *subdominant* chord. All three chords are played as major chords.

In this case the sequence runs: E D A E. If the sequence were to start in C it would run C B flat F C. What would the sequence be in the key of A major? What would it be in the key of D major?

Try writing a song of your own which uses this chord sequence.

Part of the Union

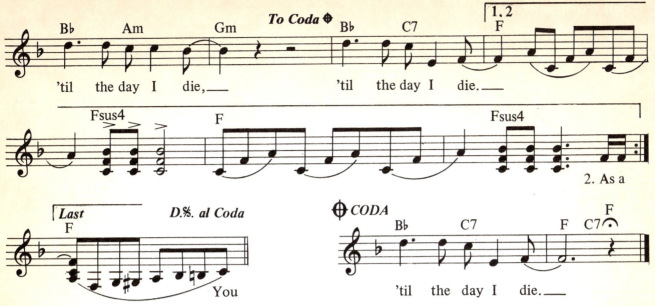

3. Before the Union did appear
   My life was half as clear,
   Now I've got the power to the working hour
   And every other day of the year.
   So though I'm a working man
   I can ruin the government's plan,
   I'm not too hard, but the sight of my card
   Makes me some kind of superman.

   CHORUS

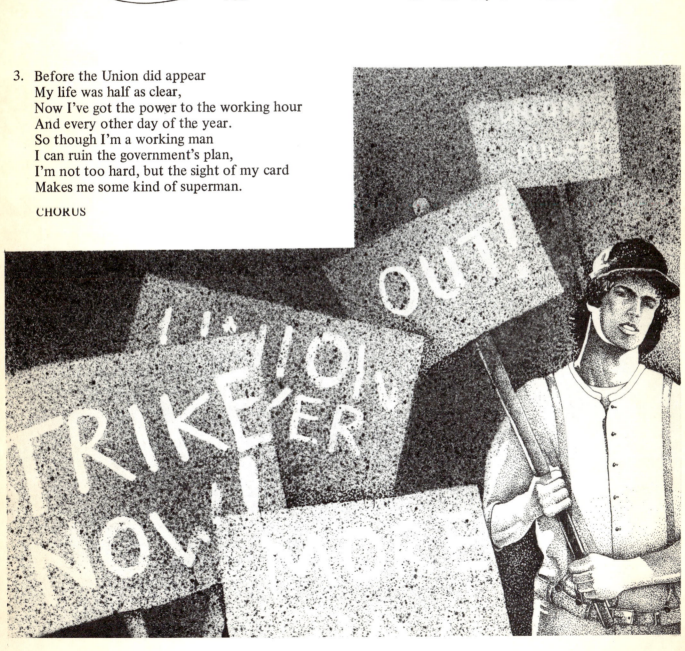

Part of the Union was a hit for the Strawbs in Britain in 1973. It got to number 2 in the charts. Soon after this success the two members of the group who wrote *Part of the Union* left to form their own band called Hudson-Ford. This left the main inspiration of Strawbs (Dave Cousins) free to continue developing the group's image on the LP market, and in fact the Strawbs have had many more hit albums than they have had hit singles.

When the record came out it caused a lot of controversy because of the unusual lyrics. Some people thought it was just a joke, whilst others saw it as an attack on trade union militants.

You'll see that at the start of the song there are four bars without words; these should be played on accompanying instruments. The same applies to the end of each verse. A separate accompaniment for a bass guitar or other bass instrument is also given.

Project

If you want to play the guitar accompaniment but are not very familiar with some of the chords played here you can put on a capo below the fifth fret and then play the accompaniment in C major. Thus every chord of F will be played as C, G minor will become D minor and so on. Work out the rest of the chords for the song to be played in C major.